T0026785

TEAM TIME MACHINE

WITNESSES

THE SIEGE

AT YORKTOWN

BY JILL KEPPELER

Gareth Stevens
PUBLISHING

Please visit our website, www.garethstevens.com. For a free color catalog of all our high-quality books, call toll free 1-800-542-2595 or fax 1-877-542-2596.

Cataloging-in-Publication Data

Names: Keppeler, Jill.
Title: Team time machine witnesses the siege at Yorktown / Jill Keppeler.
Description: New York : Gareth Stevens Publishing, 2020. | Series: Team time machine: American Revolution | Includes glossary and index.
Identifiers: ISBN 9781538246948 (pbk.) | ISBN 9781538246962 (library bound) | ISBN 9781538246955 (6 pack)
Subjects: LCSH: Yorktown (Va.)-History-Siege, 1781-Juvenile literature.
Classification: LCC E241.Y6 K46 2020 | DDC 973.3'37-dc23

First Edition

Published in 2020 by
Gareth Stevens Publishing
111 East 14th Street, Suite 349
New York, NY 10003

Designer: Katelyn E. Reynolds
Editor: Therese Shea

Photo credits: Cover, p. 1 Own work (PHGCOM), photographed in the Palais de Versailles 2009/World Imaging/ Wikipedia.org; cover, pp. 1–24 (series characters) Lorelyn Medina/Shutterstock.com; cover, pp. 1–24 (time machine elements) Agor2012/Shutterstock.com; cover, pp. 1–24 (background texture) somen/Shutterstock.com; p. 5 William Silver/ Shutterstock.com; p. 7 Hulton Archive/Getty Images; p. 9 courtesy of the Library of Congress; p. 11 Interim Archives/Getty Images; p. 13 Bettmann/Getty Images; p. 15 US Army Chief of Military Historians office, hosted ath ttp://xenophongroup. com/mcjoynt/IMAGES.HTM/Khaerr~commonswiki/Wikipedia.org; p. 19 Arne Beruldsen/Shutterstock.com; p. 21 Danita Delimont/Gallo Images/Getty Images Plus; p. 23 The Print Collector/Getty Images; p. 24 PHAS/Universal Images Group via Getty Images; p. 25 © CORBIS/Corbis via Getty Images; p. 26 Fine Art Images/Heritage Images/Getty Images; p. 27 Rotunda of the US Capitol/http://www.aoc.gov/cc/photo-gallery/ptgs_rotunda.cfm/Davepape/Wikipedia.org; p. 29 (main) Kean Collection/Getty Images; p. 29 (inset) National Archives and Records Administration, cataloged under the National Archives Identifier (NAID) 299805 (https://catalog.archives.gov/id/299805)/Diegopmc/Wikipedia.org.

Printed in the United States of America

Some of the images in this book illustrate individuals who are models. The depictions do not imply actual situations or events.

CPSIA compliance information: Batch #CW20GS: For further information contact Gareth Stevens, New York, New York at 1-800-542-2595.

CONTENTS

WORDS IN THE GLOSSARY APPEAR IN **BOLD** TYPE THE FIRST TIME THEY ARE USED IN THE TEXT.

"Gotcha!" Zoe yelled as Will ducked around the side of the school and nearly ran into her. He made a surprised noise and stopped in his tracks. He turned to go the other way—and ran right into Gaby!

"Tag!" she said, poking his shoulder. "Our team wins!"

Will laughed. "Okay, that's fair. Good teamwork! You trapped me right between you."

Zoe grinned at him. "Just like at Yorktown!" They looked at her. "Didn't you do the history reading?" she asked.

MEET TEAM TIME MACHINE

TEAM TIME MACHINE IS A GROUP OF FRIENDS WHO FOUND A TIME MACHINE ONE DAY IN A VERY ODD LIBRARY. THEY DISCOVERED THAT BOOKS FROM THE LIBRARY COULD POWER THE MACHINE AND TRANSPORT THEM TO DIFFERENT PLACES AND TIMES. IN THIS ADVENTURE, GABY, ZOE, AND WILL VISIT YORKTOWN—DURING THE AMERICAN REVOLUTION!

4

"I did the reading," Gaby told her. "But what does that have to do with it?"

"Did you look at the maps?" Zoe asked them. Zoe loved maps. "The Americans and the French trapped the British between them, just like we trapped Will."

Will looked thoughtful. "That makes what happened at Yorktown sound more interesting than just 'the place where the British **surrendered**,'" he said. "Recess is done. Let's head…"

"To the library!" the three said together.

MAPS ARE IMPORTANT TO PEOPLE PLANNING MILITARY BATTLES. IN THE AMERICAN REVOLUTION, THE SIDE WITH THE BEST MAPS HAD A BIG ADVANTAGE—AND THE BEST CHANCE FOR VICTORY!

It didn't take the friends long to find a book about the siege at Yorktown in their library. Zoe took it to the time machine and placed it inside, then looked at the others. "Ready to go?" she asked.

When they nodded, she took a deep breath and pulled the handle. The library shook and spun—and finally stopped.

"Here goes," Will whispered. He crossed to the door and peeked out, then looked back. "**Continental army** soldiers! We're in the right place."

> IT WASN'T TOO UNUSUAL TO SEE KIDS IN ARMY CAMPS DURING THE AMERICAN REVOLUTION. THEY CARRIED MESSAGES AND DID OTHER JOBS. THAT'S HOW WE BLENDED IN!

BEGINNING IN 1779, THE OFFICIAL UNIFORM OF THE CONTINENTAL ARMY BECAME A BLUE COAT WITH WHITE, RED, BLUE, OR PALE YELLOW ON THE EDGES.

The kids left the library, which now looked like a tent, and stepped into the army camp. The sun was just starting to rise. The camp was quiet, but people were moving around, preparing for the day.

Gaby ran over to ask a young soldier what day it was. She returned quickly. "It's October 15, 1781," she told Zoe and Will in a loud whisper. "Perfect!"

Will frowned. "I thought the siege of Yorktown was in September 1781?"

THE AMERICANS AND FRENCH OUTGUNNED THE BRITISH AT THE SIEGE. GENERAL CORNWALLIS WROTE, "AGAINST SO POWERFUL AN ATTACK, WE CANNOT HOPE TO MAKE A VERY LONG **RESISTANCE**."

THIS PICTURE SHOWS AMERICAN GUNS AT YORKTOWN. **CANNONS**, MORTARS, AND HOWITZERS WERE THREE KINDS OF LARGE GUNS USED THERE.

"The siege started in September and lasted into October," Zoe told him, lowering her voice. "The Americans and the French surrounded the British at Yorktown for more than 20 days. The British started to run out of food. That's one of the reasons they surrendered."

"Oh, right!" Will said, nodding. "Well, that means it should be safe enough to walk around a bit, as long as we don't get too close to the British army. We can act like we're running messages!"

YORKTOWN IS LOCATED ON A PENINSULA, WHICH IS A PIECE OF LAND ALMOST COMPLETELY SURROUNDED BY WATER. IT'S ON THE YORK RIVER NEAR CHESAPEAKE BAY.

BRITISH GENERAL CHARLES CORNWALLIS AND HIS ARMY WERE AT YORKTOWN IN PART BECAUSE HE'D BEEN ORDERED TO MAKE SURE THE BRITISH SHIPS HAD A SAFE DEEP-WATER HARBOR.

The friends walked around the camp, listening to people talk and trying to look like they were carrying important messages. The mood among the soldiers and others was good. A young drummer boy told the team that just the night before, the American and French troops had captured two small forts called redoubts that the British had built near Yorktown.

The troops had been led by the Marquis de Lafayette of France and Alexander Hamilton of the Continental army. Everyone thought the two men were very brave.

DURING THE SIEGE, A GROUP OF FRENCH SHIPS **BLOCKADED** CHESAPEAKE BAY, KEEPING CORNWALLIS AND THE BRITISH ARMY FROM ESCAPING BY WATER.

FRANCE HELPED THE CONTINENTAL ARMY WIN MANY BATTLES DURING THE AMERICAN REVOLUTION. HERE, FRENCH TROOPS ARE SHOWN ATTACKING A BRITISH REDOUBT NEAR YORKTOWN.

Meanwhile, the Continental troops were digging a second parallel. The parallel was a zigzag **trench** that would give them cover as they got closer to the British. It was only 400 yards (366 m) from the enemy position.

The kids could hear the **artillery** fire close by, so they stayed away from where the Americans and French were **bombarding** the British. Instead, they walked around and talked to people when they could. Many wondered what the **desperate** British were going to do next.

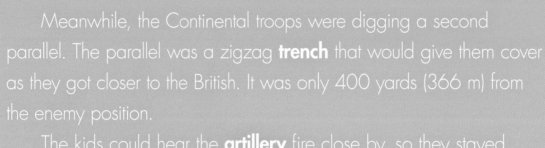

CORNWALLIS WAS WAITING FOR HELP FROM BRITISH GENERAL HENRY CLINTON, WHO WAS IN NEW YORK CITY. HOWEVER, THE SHIPS CLINTON WOULD SEND TO HELP HIM DIDN'T LEAVE NEW YORK UNTIL IT WAS TOO LATE!

YORK RIVER

FRENCH

GLOUCESTER

BRITISH FORCES

← WILLIAMSBURG

YORKTOWN

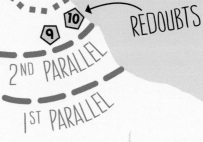

REDOUBTS

FRENCH POSITION

2ND PARALLEL

1ST PARALLEL

FIELD OF SURRENDER

WASHINGTON'S CAMP ▏

AMERICAN POSITION

Will, Zoe, and Gaby knew that they'd have to wait a few days to see the surrender at Yorktown. The drummer boy, Elias, said they could sleep in the tent he shared with his older brother, who was now a helper for one of the generals. Elias warned them that the tent had a few holes, though.

"That will be fine," Gaby told him. "It won't rain!"

"Did you *have* to say that?" Zoe sighed.

"When Gaby says that, it *always* rains!" Will explained to Elias.

> GEORGE WASHINGTON KEPT A DIARY FROM MAY TO EARLY NOVEMBER 1781. WE KNOW A LOT ABOUT WHAT HAPPENED AT YORKTOWN FROM WHAT HE WROTE.

THIS PHOTO SHOWS WHAT ONE OF THE **DEFENSIVE** LINES AT YORKTOWN WOULD HAVE LOOKED LIKE. IMAGINE TRYING TO ATTACK SOLDIERS ON THE OTHER SIDE OF THAT!

It wasn't rain that woke them early the next day, though. It was lots of people yelling! Zoe, Gaby, Will, and Elias dove out the front of the tent. The sun wasn't even up yet, but lots of soldiers were running around. Elias ran off to talk to other boys he knew, and then returned.

"The British tried to attack some of our cannons!" he said. "But we drove them back to Yorktown. We need to fix the cannons fast!"

THE BRITISH SPIKED SIX OF THE CANNONS—BUT THEY WERE FIXED BY LATER IN THE MORNING.

CORNWALLIS SENT SOLDIERS TO SPIKE SOME OF THE FRENCH AND AMERICAN CANNONS. SPIKING MEANT STOPPING THE CANNONS FROM FIRING BY DRIVING SPIKES, OR POINTY PIECES OF METAL, INTO THEM.

"I wonder what the British thought when they saw all the cannons firing again," Gaby said, holding her hands over her ears. The friends were watching the artillery line from a distance.

"I'm sure they weren't happy," Will told her. "Did you know some of the French and American soldiers are having a contest to see who can do the most harm?"

Then he looked up. "Uh oh! Those clouds look really dark . . . and listen to the wind!"

THERE WERE HUNDREDS OF CANNONS AND OTHER BIG GUNS ON THE FIELD AT YORKTOWN. THERE MIGHT HAVE BEEN AS MANY AS 400!

THIS PICTURE SHOWS GENERAL GEORGE WASHINGTON FIRING A CANNON AT THE SIEGE OF YORKTOWN. STORIES SAY HE FIRED THE FIRST SHOT.

Soon, there was an awful storm battering Yorktown. Elias's tent leaked, though the kids did their best to fix it. It was hard to sleep with the wind making so much noise. Not long after they finally fell asleep, one of Elias's friends woke them with news.

He told them that Cornwallis and his soldiers had tried to escape! They'd started sending boats across the river to Gloucester Point. But because of the storm, only a few made it.

WHEN CORNWALLIS STARTED THE ESCAPE PLAN, HE ONLY ALLOWED THE HEALTHY SOLDIERS TO GO. THE BRITISH WERE GOING TO LEAVE THEIR SICK AND HURT SOLDIERS BEHIND.

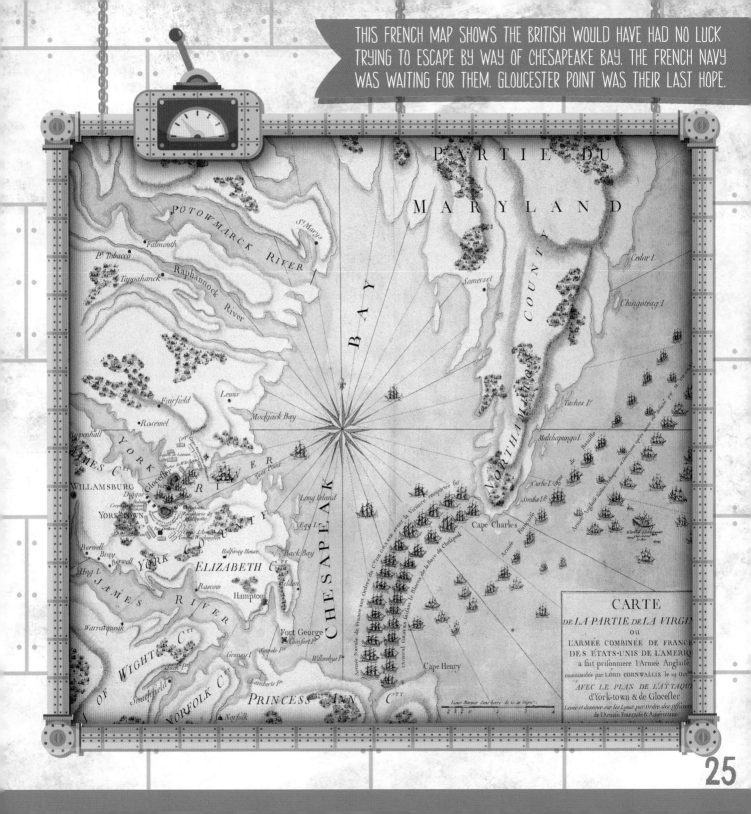

Finally, it was October 17, 1781. Team Time Machine knew what was coming! Even though they were tired, they stood in the camp the next morning and watched for signs of surrender.

"Look!" Zoe said, pointing. A drummer beating a pattern on his drum and a man with a white flag climbed to the top of the British defenses. The white flag was a sign that Cornwallis wanted the fighting to stop so the two sides could talk about the British surrender.

WITHOUT THE TEAMWORK OF THE FRENCH AND AMERICAN TROOPS AND NAVAL SHIPS, THE BRITISH MIGHT HAVE WON AT YORKTOWN. COUNT DE ROCHAMBEAU OF FRANCE HELPED PLAN THE SIEGE WITH WASHINGTON.

COUNT DE ROCHAMBEAU

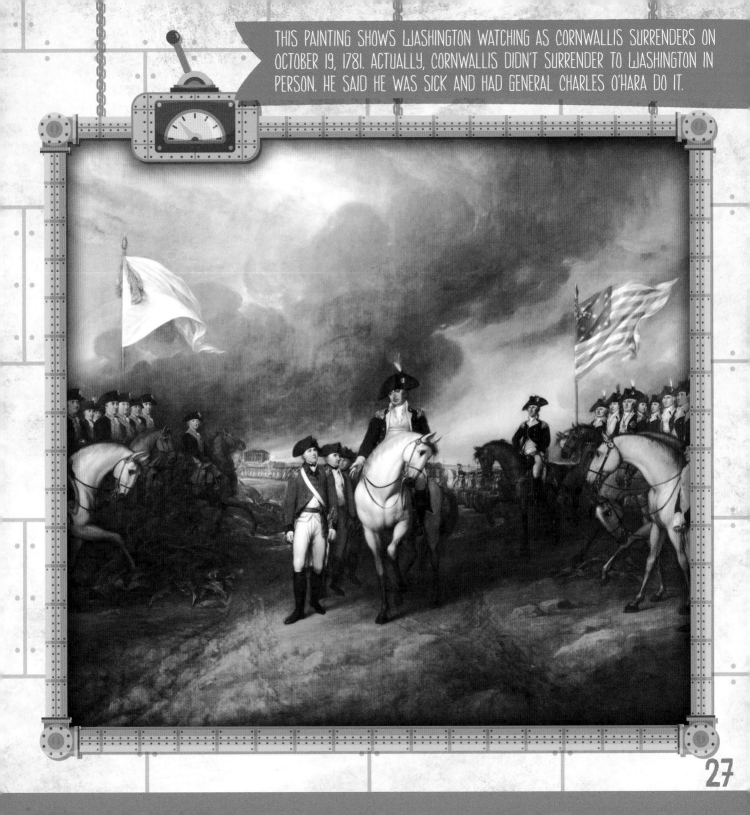

THIS PAINTING SHOWS WASHINGTON WATCHING AS CORNWALLIS SURRENDERS ON OCTOBER 19, 1781. ACTUALLY, CORNWALLIS DIDN'T SURRENDER TO WASHINGTON IN PERSON. HE SAID HE WAS SICK AND HAD GENERAL CHARLES O'HARA DO IT.

"Do you really think it's the end?" Elias whispered as he stared at the flag. "The end of the war?" The war had been fought for half his life.

"It's the beginning of the end," Zoe said. She glanced at Will and Gaby. They knew that there would still be some fighting, but most of it was over. The United States would soon be recognized as its own country.

And for Team Time Machine, it was time to go home. There were other adventures awaiting them!

MOST OF THE AMERICAN REVOLUTION WAS OVER, BUT IT WOULD STILL BE ABOUT 2 MORE YEARS BEFORE THE UNITED STATES AND ENGLAND SIGNED THE **TREATY** OF PARIS ON SEPTEMBER 3, 1783.

GLOSSARY

American Revolution: the war in which the colonies won their freedom from England

artillery: large guns that shoot shells, bullets, or missiles

blockade: to block harbors to keep people and supplies from coming and going

bombard: to attack a place with bombs, guns, and other weapons

cannon: a large gun that shoots heavy stone or metal balls

Continental army: the army of American colonists during the American Revolution, led by General George Washington

defensive: describing a way to guard against the enemy

desperate: with little to no hope

resistance: the prevention of something

siege: the use of military to surround an area or building in order to capture it

surrender: to give up, or the act of giving up

treaty: an agreement between countries

trench: a long, narrow hole dug in the ground

FOR MORE INFORMATION

BOOKS

Dugan, Christine. *Marquis de Lafayette and the French.* Huntington Beach, CA: Teacher Created Materials, 2017.

Romero, Libby. *Alexander Hamilton.* Washington, DC: National Geographic, 2018.

Thompson, Ben. *The American Revolution.* New York, NY: Little, Brown and Company, 2017.

WEBSITES

How Did the Americans Win the Revolutionary War?
www.wonderopolis.org/wonder/how-did-the-americans-win-the-revolutionary-war
Find out how the colonists won against one of the world's great powers.

Timeline of the Siege at Yorktown
www.historyisfun.org/wp-content/uploads/2018/11/Siege-of-Yorktown-Timeline.pdf
Learn more about the events at Yorktown, Virginia.

Yorktown Battlefield
www.nps.gov/york/index.htm
You can visit the site of the siege of Yorktown.

INDEX